I like the fact that the questions aren't s
They're intimate but fun at the same tim
journals feel comfortable. Good job.
T. Bruns, MN

I just moved here and the people I love most are
in Chicago. I'm sending one to my MOM, one to
my DAD, one to my GIRL and one to my MAN.
I can't wait to get them back.
S. Montiel, NJ

Very cool.
I'm anxious to read what my mom has to say
about HER teenage years.
M. Lopez, FL

Now THIS is a unique gift idea.
You really can't give or get anything
that's more personal. I would love to get one
of these from all the people I care about.
V. Dailey, AZ

I'm giving one to my dad to fill out for
my sister. Then I'll give it to my sister for
her birthday. She'll love it.
D. Brown, IL

Thank You to my family, friends, and loved ones
for your support in so many ways during the creation
of this book. I truly appreciate you all.

Let's share. This journal is dedicated to those who
seek to exchange the simplest, yet most meaningful
of gifts...the ones we carry within.

Library of Congress Cataloging-In-Publication Data available.
ISBN: 0-9720230-0-3

Sand Dune Publishing Company
P.O. Box 2995, Miller Beach, Indiana 46403
Phone: 219 938-7118   Fax 312 896-7458
email: editor@sanddunebooks.com
www.sanddunebooks.com

Words are powerful...and precious...especially when they're written by people you love. The **Between Me And You™** journal series offers a straightforward and meaningful way to get a little closer to those people.

Give it to someone you know or would like to get to know better. Inside are questions that are simple and provocative, fun to ask and fun to answer. The book is then returned to you with honest and most times, revealing responses.

Tell the recipient to have fun with it and to express themselves however they wish...with words, pictures, clippings, anything. There are also extra blank pages in the back so if you'd like to add your own VERY special questions, go for it.

On the other hand, you can tear out the pages on which there's stuff you have no need for (like this page). It's your book. And I can pretty much guarantee that this will be one you'll want to read over and over again.

And hold onto my contact information. If you get a minute, please write, call or email me and share your experience with it. Thanks.

                                                            Winston

between me and you™
MOM

This book belongs to _____

and was given to my Mom, _____

She put up with my questions and

returned it to me on _____

between me and you™

MOM

Hi Mom.

I'm giving this book to you so that you'll return it to me. You're so very special and this is my chance to learn a little more about who you WERE once upon a time and who you ARE right now.

It's funny how all who touch us affect our lives in unique ways. Especially parents.

Please take some time and reflect on the questions inside and write as much or as little as you want.

I look forward to getting this back soon. And please know that I will cherish it, not because of what you write, but simply because you wrote.

Thanks.

Contents

When You Were A Kid

What do you remember most
about being a kid?

What were some of your favorite
things *to do* as a child?

What are your favorite memories
of your father?

conversations

when you were a kid

What are some of your favorite memories of
your **mother** *?*

characteristics

What was your sister(s) like when you were growing up?

*What was your **brother**(s) like*
when you were growing up?

decisions

when you were a kid

Did you ever get upset *with your parents?*
Why?

Do you remember your
childhood friends?
What are your memories?

school

neighborhood

when you were a kid

teachers

when you were a kid

What kind of **student** *were you as a kid?*

What were your favorite subjects?

why

when you were a kid

When you were a kid,
what did you want to be when you
grew up?

Your Youth

peer pressure

What are your memories of being

a teenager?

So...what were your teenage
           dating *experiences? Do you*
remember your first date?

crushes

first kiss

Did you have any role models
when you were a teen? Who were they
and why did you look up to them?

heroes

heroines

stars

your youth

songs

your youth

What kind of music *did you like as a teen?*
Any favorite artists or groups?

Did you have a dream or burning desire
to have any particular experience or
adventure *as a young adult?*

travels

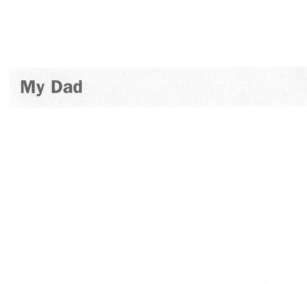

My Dad

Tell me about the first time
you *met* Dad.

Do you remember the first time
you and dad went out?
                    Tell me about it.

How long did you go out with dad?

Any memorable experiences?

places

my dad

Was marriage always part of your plan?

How did it happen?

wedding

Which have been the most interesting
times during your life with dad?

thrills

What About Me?

(my favorite part)

feelings

what about me?

*What do you remember most
about the time you
were pregnant with me?*

What are your memories of

the day I was **born?**

people

the wait

weather

what about me?

toys

Do you have any favorite memories of me as a child?

Was there anything that I did as I was
growing up that reminded you
of yourself as a child?

skills

attitudes

personality

What interests and characteristics
have you seen in me
that you also had once upon a time?

What characteristics do you think you and I share now?

How do you think we are

different?

What do you think is my
best quality?

What do you think is my
not-so-best quality?

So far, have I turned out pretty much
the way you expected I would?
Any surprises?

values

What more would you like to see me
do or **learn** *in this lifetime?*

You, Now

events

people

you, now

What really, really, really makes you

happy?

What are some of the things
you would still like to
accomplish?

relationships

challenges

Do you have any future plans
that you would care to share with me?

dreams

goals

Tell me about the **work** *you've done throughout your life.*

fun

profit

voluntary

you, now

What do you think is your best quality?

*What do you think is your **worst** quality?*

As you think about your life so far, what

are you most proud of ?

talents

occasions

*Do you have **any** regrets*
that you'd care to share with me?

near

you, now

What have been your favorite travels?
Any interesting stories?

Is there anything you think I should know *about anything? Anything at all?*
Anything?

anything

you, now

If you felt the need to offer some advice
to me, what would it be?

wisdom

you, now

Other Stuff

other stuff

other stuff

other stuff

other stuff

other stuff

I know I've asked a lot of questions. Thanks for taking the time...

and for being real.